~ FIRST GREEK MYTHS ~
THESEUS AND THE MAN-EATING MONSTER

To Victor Agius
S.P.

To all my boys
J.L.

ORCHARD BOOKS
338 Euston Road, London NW1 3BH
Orchard Books Australia
Level 17/207 Kent Street, Sydney NSW 2000
This text was first published in the form of a gift collection
called *First Greek Myths* by Orchard Books in 2003
This edition first published in hardback by Orchard Books in 2007
First paperback publication in 2008
Text © Saviour Pirotta 2007
Cover illustrations © Jan Lewis 2007
Inside Illustrations © Jan Lewis 2007
The rights of Saviour Pirotta to be identified as the author and
of Jan Lewis to be identified as the illustrator of this work
have been asserted by them in accordance with the
Copyright, Designs and Patents Act, 1988.
A CIP catalogue record for this book is available from the British Library.
ISBN 978 1 84616 472 9 (hardback)
ISBN 978 1 84616 770 6 (paperback)
1 3 5 7 9 10 8 6 4 2 (hardback)
1 3 5 7 9 10 8 6 4 2 (paperback)
Orchard Books is a division of Hachette Children's Books,
an Hachette Livre UK company.
Printed in China

www.orchardbooks.co.uk

~ FIRST GREEK MYTHS ~
'HESEUS AND THE MAN-EATING MONSTER

BY SAVIOUR PIROTTA
ILLUSTRATED BY JAN LEWIS

ORCHARD BOOKS

~ CAST LIST ~

THESEUS,
a handsome prince

ARIADNE,
a princess

King Minos of Crete was an evil king. He had a huge maze under his palace where he kept a monster called the Minotaur.

The Minotaur was half man and half bull. King Minos fed it on humans.

Every year, the King of Athens had to send seven men and seven women for the Minotaur or King Minos would make war on Athens.

Now the King of Athens had a son called Theseus. One day, Theseus said to his father, "We have to stop this happening. Let me go and kill the beast."

"Then take this white sail for your ship," said the King.

"If you kill the Minotaur, hang it on the mast. Then I will know you are coming home alive."

Theseus was a brave man but he was not very clever. When he arrived in Crete, King Minos's guards led him to the entrance of the maze.

They removed his sword and
left him. Now, even if he did
manage to kill the beast, how
would he find his way out?

Theseus thought he heard someone whispering his name.

Then, before him, he saw Ariadne, one of King Minos's daughters.

"Here," she said, handing Theseus a sword and a ball of wool. "You take the ball and I'll hold the end. When you want to come back out of the maze, all you have to do is wind it up."

"But why do you want to help me?" asked Theseus.

"I don't like living here," said Ariadne. "I want you to take me to Athens and marry me."

It sounded like a fair deal to
Theseus so he started to make
his way through the dark,
winding maze.

As Theseus felt his way down the passages, he knew the Minotaur was close behind.

Then, suddenly, a loud bellow made him jump.

At the far end of the corridor, a pair of glowing, red eyes were staring at him.

Theseus thought about the people the monster had eaten and that made him brave and angry. "Come on," he shouted. "Come and get your supper."

The Minotaur roared and started running towards him. Theseus waited until he was nearly face to face with the monster and then he stepped sideways.

The Minotaur grunted angrily
and lurched towards Theseus
again. But the young man was
too quick.

All night long the two chased
each other around the maze.

At last the Minotaur started to
tire. Theseus jumped forward and
drove his sword straight into its
heart. The monster roared, then
crashed to the ground.

Quickly, Theseus rolled up the
wool and made his way out of
the maze.

"Follow me!" cried Ariadne.
She led him through a secret
passage out of the palace.
Soon they were on board
Theseus's ship.

On the way home, they stopped at an island. There, Theseus tricked Ariadne and sailed on without her. Now that he had killed the Minotaur he had changed his mind about marrying her.

Theseus ordered a feast for his men.

During the celebrations, the ship came within sight of Athens, but Theseus had forgotten to put up his father's white sail in place of the usual black one.

27

When the king saw it, he
thought his son was dead. Mad
with grief, he threw himself into
the deep sea.

Theseus was heartbroken. If
only he had put up the white sail.
But it was too late. His father was
dead, gone forever.

A few days later, Theseus was crowned the new king.

"From now on," he promised his people, "I shall never do anything rash or foolhardy again."

~ FIRST GREEK MYTHS ~
THESEUS AND THE MAN-EATING MONSTER

BY SAVIOUR PIROTTA ⌐ ILLUSTRATED BY JAN LEWIS

And enjoy a little magic with these First Fairy Tales:

First Greek Myths and First Fairy Tales are available from all
good bookshops,or can be ordered direct from the publisher:
Orchard Books, PO BOX 29, Douglas IM99 1BQ
Credit card orders please telephone 01624 836000
or fax 01624 837033
or e-mail: bookshop@enterprise.net for details.

To order please quote title, author and ISBN
and your full name and address.
Cheques and postal orders should be
made payable to 'Bookpost plc'.
Postage and packing is FREE within the UK
(overseas customers should add £1.00 per book).

Prices and availability are subject to change.